My Feelings and Me

By Holde Kreul
Illustrated by Dagmar Geisler

Sky Pony Press
New York

Sky Pony Press books may be purchased in bulk at special discounts for sales promotion, corporate gifts, fund-raising, or educational purposes. Special editions can also be created to specifications. For details, contact the Special Sales Department, Sky Pony Press, 307 West 36th Street, 11th Floor, New York, NY 10018 or info@skyhorsepublishing.com.

Sky Pony® is a registered trademark of Skyhorse Publishing, Inc.®, a Delaware corporation.
Visit our website at www.skyponypress.com.

10 9 8 7 6 5 4 3 2

Manufactured in China, December 2017
This product conforms to CPSIA 2008

Library of Congress Cataloging-in-Publication Data is available on file.

Cover design by Kate Gartner
Cover illustration by Dagmar Geisler

Print ISBN: 978-1-5107-3533-0
Ebook ISBN: 978-1-5107-3535-4

Dear Grown-ups,

Children often do not know how to deal with their emotions. They orient themselves toward adults, who usually hide their feelings.

Adults often judge children's feelings very quickly, and sometimes even punish rage and jealousy, treating them as negative feelings. As a result, children learn that it can be very problematic and unpleasant to show their emotions. They begin to cover them up and suppress them, which in turn restricts and limits their personalities.

Feelings are also always involved in our relationships with other people, so children must develop their own emotions in order to be able react to the emotions of others. Being aware of our own emotions and dealing with them responsibly is important for living together successfully. The extent to which we control our feelings or give them free rein is a learning process and a trial of limits.

This book invites you to the conversation. It gives children the opportunity to confront their own feelings, to recognize themselves, and to examine their own reactions. It also provides encouragement to stand up for all emotions.

Holde Kreul

It is good to know my feelings and show them!

When I am very happy, I can laugh loudly and shout with glee.

When I'm cranky and angry,
I can scream and roar.

When I love someone, I can hug them and cuddle with them.

When I'm sad, sometimes I have to cry.

When I'm afraid, I want
to hole up and hide.

When I am jealous of someone, my feelings fight inside me. I am disappointed and mad at the same time.

Sometimes a feeling gets stronger and stronger.

When I'm frightened, I freeze up and lose all my confidence. Then it feels good when someone takes my hand and gives me courage.

Sometimes I stomp on the floor in rage, or I break something. Then no one can get too close to me.

When I'm furious, I feel uncomfortable,
and I'm afraid nobody will like me anymore.
But my loved ones me like me anyway.
Because sometimes they feel the same way.

I can hurt others with my feelings, especially when I am angry or jealous. But when I argue with or upset someone, I can also make up with them afterward. Sometimes that is hard to do, though, because I am ashamed.

When I show my feelings, I am no longer alone with them.

Others can celebrate along with me when I'm happy.

Others can comfort me and talk to me about what's wrong when I'm sad.

Because I know my own feelings,
I can often understand other
people's feelings, too. It's nice to
feel that I can help others.

Understanding feelings also helps me say, "Stop!" when someone lashes out in anger.

I do not always want to show what I feel. Especially not when I'm afraid I'll be laughed at or not taken seriously. Then I act as if I don't feel anything.

Sometimes others can see how I feel even if I do not want them to . . .

Because I blush red when I'm ashamed.

Or because I tremble when I'm afraid.

When my heart pounds loudly because I am very nervous, no one can see. Only I can feel that.

Sometimes others want to talk away
my feelings. They say:
"You're such a scaredy-cat!" if I am afraid.
"Don't worry about it!" when I'm sad.
"Pull yourself together!" when I'm angry.
But my feelings are still there.

There are days when my feelings are a jumbled mess.

When Mom and Dad scold me, I'm annoyed and cranky—but I still love them.

Or when I'm crying and don't really know why. Then it is nice if someone takes me in their arms.

We all have many feelings.

Some are wonderful, and some are more difficult. But they all belong to us—just like our noses or our hands do. And that's a nice feeling.

Holde Kreul is a German author. She studied psychology and has been working with children for her whole career. For a long time, she directed a day-care center for children with mental disorders. Today she has her own psychotherapeutic practice and works with children and adults.

Dagmar Geisler is a German author and illustrator. She studied graphic design at the University of Applied Sciences in Wiesbaden and worked for several publishing houses and broadcasting companies. Today, Dagmar focuses mainly on children's books, both as an illustrator and an author. She illustrated *My Body Belongs to Me from My Head to My Toes* which received the Silver Feather (*Silberne Feder*) Children's Book Prize from the German Medical Women's Association, and is the author/illustrator of *I Won't Go With Strangers*. She lives with her family in Switzerland.